ALSO BY JOHN LEHMAN

POETRY

Shrine of the Tooth Fairy

Dogs Dream of Running

Shorts, Brief Wisconsin Poems

NON-FICTION

Make Good Writing Great

The Zen of Sales & Marketing

FICTION

Take

America's Greatest Unknown Poet

Lorine Niedecker
Reminiscences, Photographs, Letters
and Her Most Memorable Poems

Poet of place, Lorine loved her river-island world.

America's Greatest Unknown Poet

**Lorine Niedecker
Reminiscences, Photographs, Letters
and Her Most Memorable Poems**

by John Lehman

Foreword by R. Virgil Ellis

Zelda Wilde Publishing   Cambridge, Wisconsin   2003

Book design by Tom Pomplun.
Printed in the United States of America.

Library of Congress Cataloging-in-Publication Data
Lehman, John. 1941 — 1st ed.
America's Greatest Unknown Poet: Lorine Niedecker
ISBN 0-9741728-0-4
I. Poetry, American II.Title. III. Biography.
IV. Literary Criticism V. Author

*To Tom Pomplun and Rod Clark for the many years we have worked together making **Rosebud** a reality.*

Contents

Acknowledgments

John Lehman would like to thank Cid Corman, Jenny Penberthy, Bonnie Roub, Carl Gartung, Tom Pomplun, Ron Ellis, Bob Wake, Rod Clark, Talia Schorr, Georgene Pomplun and Marilla Fuge for their help and support, and also Gnomon Press, Cambridge University Press, National Poetry Foundation, Duke University Press and the Jargon Society for permission to use Niedecker excerpts from their publications. Faith B. Miracle's assistance with proofing and editing was invaluable. Dave Bruns, a generous and considerate Wisconsin businessman, deserves special recognition. Without his support this book would not have been possible.

Foreword

"So You've Found Me Out!"

NOT FAR FROM Lorine Niedecker's home on Blackhawk Island there's a road bearing her parents' family name: Kunz (her maternal grandparents). Although I lived on that road for several years before her death, I never associated the name with her. Nor did I understand her importance as a poet when I made her acquaintance in 1966. That was the year my family and I moved to Wisconsin, penniless and loaded with debts incurred during my three years of graduate work at Cornell University. Caring for four very young children, studying intensively for the Ph.D. comprehensives and becoming involved in the antiwar and voter registration movements pretty well guaranteed that I wouldn't be able to spend much time with a reclusive poet, let alone try to write poetry of my own. Nevertheless my brother Herbert, who taught in a Fort Atkinson school, urged me to see her, and so I did, paying her two or three visits in late 1966. It was only in subsequent years that it slowly dawned on me that I'd been privileged to briefly know one of the great modern writers, a realization with some sense of an opportunity missed.

"So you've found me out!" were the first words Lorine Niedecker spoke when I met her. She struck me as unassuming, austere and vibrant, at home and quite alone in the sparsely furnished cottage. Her husband Al, she explained, was often in Milwaukee or busy with projects in a small adjoining workshop. Although not a large person, she had a presence, alertness and a confidence that contradicts the view that she was "tiny" and "timid." As we talked I quickly became aware that Lorine Niedecker was far more knowledgeable than I was about poetry, and indeed, about many writers in general.

Sitting with Lorine on the floor of her little house, I watched her reach for books from the low shelves and was delighted to see her passion for literature. She was pleased that I knew of Zukofsky and the Objectivist movement (an avant-garde approach that regards the poem as an object apart from its meaning, paying more attention to its images and structure than to a theme it might convey). She laughed approvingly when I quoted William Carlos Williams's famous adage, "no ideas but in things." But it didn't take long for my flash-card level of expertise to bottom out. She moved easily from Basho to Zukofsky and spoke of her interest in Freud and Jung, Darwin and Swedenborg. Knowing I was an aspiring poet, she recommended numerous books and showed me copies of *Origin*, a little magazine edited for many years by Cid Corman. She read a few of her poems form *New Goose* and *My Friend Tree*, and tried to tell me about her poetics — how she had moved from what she called "my untamed surrealism" to focus on the image…to be more objective.

I wasn't so sure about the importance of Objectivism. I didn't like much of Olson, Creeley, Duncan; I liked very little of Zukofsky. In fact there weren't many poems of Lorine's that I liked. Although I took this emphasis on imagery in stride because Pound and many others had made the case to "make it new," I didn't care for poetry that shook off traditional ways in which words, phrases and clauses were put together. The best modern poetry, it seemed to me, had succeeded by *using* the resources of syntax rather than dismissing them. The case made by writers such as Donald Davie in *Articulate Energy: An Inquiry into the Syntax of English Poetry* proved convincing. Imagism, and Objectivism after it, had taken Pound's fascinations too far. What works in an Eastern language which uses pictures or symbols to represent ideas doesn't work well in a Western one. There can never be genuine haiku in English because word-order, syntax, is intrinsic to the language and carries its own energy.

Evidently it was not easy for Niedecker to write non-syntactically: "For me the sentence lies in wait — all those prepositions and connectives — like an early spring flood. A good thing my follow-up feeling has always been condense, condense…" The term "condensery," from her poem *Poet's Work*, is well known as the key term in understanding her style. The process was evidently laborious; it was not always easy for her to finish her poems. In poem *XIV* of *For Paul, Group Two* she says, "What would they say if they knew / I sit for two months on six lines / of poetry?" But the advantages of "condensing" are familiar to us in praises of Cid Corman and others. Corman states, "Her haiku-like brief poems are as fine as any short poems of our or any time." Kenneth Cox says, "...the best of her poems do without devices altogether. Simple in appearance and sparing in expression, they convey a manifold meaning beyond the reach of analysis..." and Michael Heller concludes, "It is an objective, yet human magic which makes her poems seem as organic as the experiences they arise from, resonating with pure being rather than with associations."

Of course there are risks that the "condensing" process hazards, the worst of which is to alienate the reader. As Lorine herself put it in a letter to Corman, "The hard and clear with the mystery of poetry and it's done largely by the words omitted. Stark, isolated words which must somehow connect with each other and into the next line and the sense out of the sound." Without the energy of verbs, perhaps the most-omitted syntactic elements (especially linking verbs) in Niedecker's poetry, and with frequent ellipses, the likelihood increases that a reader will be left behind, as I felt I was at my first acquaintance with her work. Even the best-liked and most-quoted poems left me puzzled and rather frustrated. Consider this line, "Remember my little granite pail?" I couldn't imagine a pail made of granite. Wouldn't it be unwieldy? A quick look in the dictionary showed that the correct term is "graniteware," referring to enameled ironware. Was the pail then made of iron, which would have to be cast iron, unless it were steel? Wasn't that unlikely for a "little" pail? Why not admit that the pail was enameled steel, or tin? Of course changing any word would do violence to the fit of all the words in this poem. The importance of "granite" may be that its unorthodox use shows the genius of a poet who, in concert with the Muse, is creating art that will "carry me through."

When Lorine, in a letter to me, quoted some short haiku-like poems by Keith Owen, she wrote: "Japanese influence, of course. Ever felt it? I am perhaps ending with that influence. Perhaps everyone should begin with it." I wasn't so sure. I wanted *all* the resources of the language available in my toolkit. It was no wonder that in addition to encouraging me she also, with great delicacy, deprecated my "rather tight-logical-hard thought manner." And in another letter she said, "I could not 'take flight' from your poems but I admire the hard, sober, sincere, *weight*." Her advice was characteristically modest: "I always tell everybody including myself: fewer words, more quiet and pay attention to spaces as well as words! But who am I to tell anybody?" Gradually I realized that my problems with her poetry stemmed from my own literal-mindedness and that she was more than a few jumps ahead of me.

I remember between visits trying to come to grips with my coolness toward Lorine's poetry, the very brevity of it. Donald Davie writes of the "lyric minimum" of *Lake Superior* as troubling the reader: "Faced with such daunting or taunting brevities, our first impulse is to annotate. Sometimes the impulse should be resisted, and certainly it shouldn't be indulged at length. But in this case some annotation cannot be avoided." Davie contrasts Janet Lewis's dramatic description of a Great Lakes ore ship as "a very striking and instructive contrast to Niedecker's blank, almost perfunctory 'big boats / coal-black and iron-ore-red / topped with what white castle work.'" He also makes it clear that such a minimal approach can distort our perspective. Both Lewis and Niedecker portray the ethnologist Henry Rowe Schoolcraft; Lewis with a full account of Schoolcraft's racism, and Niedecker with the terse "Schoolcraft left the Soo...for Minnesota." The problem is that the "Indians, the indigenous and original inhabitants of the Lake Superior region, don't figure in Niedecker's poem at all, except as the savages who tore out poor Radisson's finger-nails." Davie excuses Lorine, however, on the grounds that her poem's time-frame is geological—the minerals of the Lake Superior region are in a real sense the only true "heroes" of the poem.

Lorine was well aware that she was pushing the envelope, parenthetically noting to Corman that "Basho himself must have been very complex." In spite of self-doubt, and by virtue of an appreciation for her contemporaries, she persisted. She wrote: "I've been going through a bad time, in one moment (winter) I'd have thrown over all my (if one can) years of clean-cut, concise short poem manner for 'something else' (still don't know what to call it)...but a glimpse at the work of Koch and Ashbery and I'm quite sure I've been doing OK for a long time." Not that doing OK was easy.

Perhaps a writer must counter self-doubt with a sense of the rightness of his or her own artistic strategy and the wrongness or inadequacy of that of others. But poetry comprises a wide kingdom: there will always be a polarity between a full and flowing, syntax-rich style and a spare, minimal, lapidary. The hard-won firmness of Lorine's perspective is prominent in her poems and letters, as it was in her conversations with me. From that frame she could write of my own poetry, "...there is every indication of a great ease, a flexible flowing style is being developed...you are a careful writer but *restrained*, O very, it is natural you shd [sic] feel the machine thing in our society but you will get out from under..." I like to think that in some measure I have, though perhaps not altogether in the way she would have preferred. Now, over thirty years later, as I recover my memories and re-discover Lorine, I'm thankful for her willingness to visit, the warmth she gave to the plain white cottage and for her advice. Now when I drive on Kunz Road where my daughter currently lives, I remember Lorine, grateful that I spent some time in her presence. Today, readers of her words will feel the same.

—R. Virgil Ellis, July 2003

Timeline

Lorine Niedecker's Life

May 12, 1903	Lorine Faith Niedecker is born to Henry (Hank) and Theresa (Daisy) Kunz, Fort Atkinson, Wisconsin
June 1922	Graduates from Fort Atkinson High School
Sept. 1922 – 23	Attends Beloit College, Beloit, Wisconsin
May 1928 – Aug. 1930	Works as a librarian's assistant at the Dwight Foster Public Library in Fort Atkinson, Wisconsin
Nov. 29, 1928	Marries Frank Hartwig. By 1930 they have permanently separated and she returns to her parents' home
1931	Reads Zukofsky's Objectivist issue of *Poetry* and, six months later, writes him, initiating their long-term correspondence
1934	Goes to New York to meet Louis Zukofsky
1938 – 1942	Lives in Madison, Wisconsin and works as a writer, then research editor for the Federal Writers' Project. Briefly serves as a radio scriptwriter for WHA Public Radio
1942	Returns to Blackhawk Island and files for a divorce from Frank Hartwig
1946	*New Goose* is published
May 8, 1944 – June 14, 1950	Proofreader at Hoard's, publisher of *Hoard's Dairyman*; she has her own house built on the banks of the Rock River
1947	Visits the Zukofskys in New York

July 1951	Daisy Niedecker dies
1953	(Christmas) Visits the Zukofskys in New York
1954	Henry Niedecker dies
Feb. 1957– late 1963	Works at the Fort Atkinson Memorial Hospital cleaning kitchens
1961	*My Friend Tree* is published
May 26, 1963	Marries Albert Millen, moves to Milwaukee in March 1964
1965	(Summer) Trip to South Dakota
1966	*Origin* (July 1966) features Niedecker
Feb. 8, 1967	Jonathan Williams visits her and in July, Basil Bunting
May 1968	Meets the Zukofskys in Madison, Wisconsin
July 1968	Trip to Minnesota and North Dakota
Dec. 1968	*North Central* is published
Aug. 1968	Retires permanently to Blackhawk Island
1969	*T & G* is published and the next year enlarged with the title *My Life by Water*
Nov. 15, 1970	Cid and Shizumi Corman visit
Dec. 31, 1970	Lorine Niedecker dies

Lorine Niedecker (age nine) was an only child.

Chapter One

Enough to Carry Me Thru

I have a story, too, that unfolds and grows only in my dreams. I can't even remember it now. It never happens in waking life only in dreams and while I'm adding to it in sleep I realize that I'm composing and think of myself as quite a genius. What a life!
— from a letter to Louis Zukofsky, 1948

LORINE NIEDECKER LIVED MUCH OF HER LIFE beside a flooding river in a barren cottage without electricity or running water. She worked as a cleaning woman scrubbing floors in a hospital and, unknown to most who came in contact with her, wrote fierce poetry. Today she's included in the *Norton Anthology* alongside such literary giants as Emily Dickinson and William Carlos Williams.

At the heart of her story is the relationship of writing and reading to the life she lived and the place where she lived it. Her words and those of people she knew raise questions for all of us. "What can we achieve through writing?" "How are we affected by where we live?" "Who inspires us?" "Why is a piece of writing great?" We need to determine the answers to these questions for ourselves, but Lorine Niedecker's life and work provide a unique touchstone that enables us to do this. Strictly speaking, this book is neither a biography nor a critical appraisal of Lorine Niedecker's work. Rather it's more like a documentary (in very loose chronological order) that allows us to draw our own conclusions — a documentary about a little-known poet whose greatness may be that her struggles reflect our own.

Let's begin with the words of a neighbor.

"I remember my astonishment when Lorine Niedecker's lawyer asked me if I knew that I had a neighbor who was a published poet. He set up a meeting for us in the new house she and Al Millen had just built and we became immediate and lasting friends. I was thirty-eight, she sixty-one...

"At first we spoke mainly about high water and the neighbors and public events— these were the Johnson years and we were both

Kennedy Democrats — and a natural modesty would have prevented her from pushing her poems at me. I was interested in the poetry, but it was not easy to find. There were just the two early books, *My Friend Tree* and *New Goose*, and when I did get hold of some of the poems I at first found them cryptic, but I would grow out of that.

"She knew I was interested. I think she sensed my difficulties, and as trust grew between us she decided to allow me in some ways to share the privacy of her artistic life. I had probably known her about a year when I suddenly and directly asked her, 'Lorine, who are you?' Her reply, equally direct, showed that she understood exactly what I wanted to know: 'William Carlos Williams said that I am the Emily Dickinson of my time.' After that I began to try harder…

"We lost Lorine very suddenly in December 1970. I had not seen her for a couple of months and was unaware of the dramatic change in her health. Cid Corman noted that she was shaking visibly when he visited her in November, days before her fatal illness. A heart condition and high blood pressure led to a stroke, from which she never recovered. Fortunately, she had left a copy of her poem on Darwin in my mailbox or we would not have been aware of a true version of the poem until much later. Corman's only version was one he had transcribed from a tape recording of Lorine reading the poem. Not until this less accurate version appeared in Corman's collection, called *Blue Chicory*, did I realize that I had an obligation to make contact with those who were guarding Lorine's legacy.

"Today as I write I can hear Canada geese flying over Fort Atkinson, and it immediately makes me think of Blackhawk Island, where I spent ten of my happiest years living in a wonderful little house remodeled from my grandfather's fishing shack. The 'island' — really a peninsula — is narrow and low, and one is always aware of shimmering water, except on a very still day or in winter, when all liquid motion stops. My living room was so close to the river that sunlight reflected off the choppy surface and made a happy dancing light on the walls and ceiling. When the moon did this same trick it was worth turning off the lights to watch. 'What a wonderful house!' said Lorine the first time she stepped in and saw her beloved river framed by the big windows — and across the river a wildness that had changed little from the days when Marquette and the French voyageurs came this way.

"On a summer night you could fall asleep to a great horned owl's distant trumpet or the din of frogs in the marsh across the road. I knew the place as a child, because we often spent summer months there, but for Lorine it was her first and lasting awareness of reality, the glass through which she saw and interpreted the world. She wrote me about this in a letter from Milwaukee, how place was inseparable from her poetry and her being.

"Lorine was preoccupied in the summer of 1967 with an attempt to define herself as a poet and apparently felt her writing could not be easily categorized. As she thought about it, writing her letter, she came up with the word 'reflective.'

"Now that I'm into Lorine's poetry, now that I've read and reread the reviews and pored over her letters, how I wish I could have a good visit with her and ask her what she may have had in mind for this or that line of poetry. As I think back — and now it's twenty-four years later — she was more than ready to tell me. If only I had pressed the button on a tape recorder and just let her talk. These are not small regrets, but they pale beside the richness Lorine has brought to me and Bonnie. She seems very near, and we know her better all the time."

— Gail Roub, 1994

———

Remember my little granite pail?
The handle of it was blue.
Think what's got away in my life—
Was enough to carry me thru.

———

An early associate, Edwin Honig, talks about Lorine's middle-aged years.

"She was born in 1903, and so — like my mother, born slightly before her — on the brink of the twentieth century. When I knew Lorine best, in 1938–39, she was about thirty-five and I was nearing twenty. What brought us together was the WPA Federal Writers' Project in Madison, Wisconsin where I had a job that kept me going at least eighteen months into the fall of 1939.

"For me the time was both peculiarly free and oppressive. In the bitterly cold winter of 1935–36 I had come, almost penniless, from New York City on a Greyhound bus, lugging a big black cardboard suitcase and hoping to enroll at the University. I was exhilarated by the prospect of finding a part-time job that would sustain me for a while in what was widely known as the most progressive university in the country...

"Then, through the intercession of a cashiered college instructor, who became head of the Writers' Project, I was taken on as a junior writer at eighty-four dollars a month. There I met and quickly became friends with Lorine on the basis of our interest in poetry (She was a senior writer, making perhaps ninety-two a month!).

"A slight, almost frail woman, she walked with quick short steps. Bifocals made her milky blue eyes seem larger than they were. Her hair was ashen blonde and wispy; the thickness of her lips made them look large as well. Her laugh was spontaneous and sudden, but quickly suppressed with one hand clapped over her mouth, her head averted. She had a good wit, a high-pitched girlish voice and a strong sense of the incongruous, which made her a good storyteller. Anecdotes she told concerned country people, her mother, father and neighbors back home in Fort Atkinson...

"Few of those on the Project were practicing writers; most were distraught housewives, clerks and displaced librarians. In her own work as a poet, Lorine felt vitally connected with poetry in the [Ezra] Pound school—in Great Britain, with Ronald Duncan, Basil Bunting, Hugh MacDiarmid. But her special guide and mentor remained, as always, Louis Zukofsky. She assiduously exchanged letters with him, and I was much impressed with the degree that she counted on his words as a source of living sustenance—even going beyond Louis to his wife, Celia, and to their young son, Paul. From Lorine and indirectly from Zukofsky, I suppose, I learned about "open forms," the work of the Objectivists, Williams and of course Pound, and then indirectly again, of the poetry of social consciousness. It seemed pretty clear that most of Lorine's reading of poetry, science, politics and music theory came directly from Zukofsky and Pound, a paideuma I was not ready to follow...

"In some way I continue to wish I might have learned more from her. But we were evolving in different orbits. Her work improved vastly, as Cid Corman pointed out, after 1940. Her preoccupations were taking her more deeply inward to the rich vein in her last years from which she drew her best poems. Mine were taking me farther outward to a life and a world that seemed increasingly antithetical to writing poetry. But I continued to write, and am glad to have been able to survive into a time which has begun to honor Lorine, the grace of her spirit, her superb gift, at last."

— Edwin Honig, 1996

And here is a glimpse of Lorine's life from her own letters and four of her poems — the first two from the perspective of her mother:

Was shoveling snow the other morning at 5:30 when big round moon was almost setting—just like night, bright moonlight, lovely [ ]. I burn my trash (waste from flood) on path to river in a spot bare of snow. Nights I bend over the porch filling my small oil can to fill oil heater. I go to folks for my drinking water as my own well water isn't clear yet— I'm not home enough to pump it to the stage fit for using. Drafty errands in becky (outhouse), sharp but fair—love it all. An egg froze for me in my box on the porch but ate it anyway. A bit of life in the country, wut?

— from a letter to Zukofsky, 1947

———

Well, spring overflows the land
floods floor, pump, wash machine
of the woman moored to this low shore by deafness.

   Good-bye to lilacs by the door
   and all I planted for the eye.
   If I could hear — too much talk in the world,
   too much wind washing, washing
   good black dirt away.

Her hair is high.
Big blind ears.

   I've wasted my whole life in water.
   My man's got nothing but leaky boats.
   My daughter, writer, sits and floats.

———

Lorine talked to her deaf mother through writing.

———

What horror to awake at night
and in the dimness see the light.
      Time is white
      mosquitoes bite
I've spent my life on nothing.

The thought that stings. How are you, Nothing,
sitting around with Something's wife.
      Buzz and burn
      is all I learn
I've spent my life on nothing.
I'm pillowed and padded, pale and puffing
lifting household stuffing —
      carpets, dishes
      benches, fishes
I've spent my life in nothing.

———

My father said "I remember
a warm Thanksgiving Day
we shipped seine
without coats
nudged 20,000 lbs. of barged buffalo fish
thru the mouth of the river
by balmy moonlight
other times
you laid out with your hands glazed
to the nets."

———

The clothesline post is set
yet no totem-carvings distinguish the Niedecker tribe
from the rest; every seventh day they wash:
worship sun; fear rain, their neighbors' eyes;
raise their hands from ground to sky,
and hang or fall by the whiteness of their all.

———

Had Pa and Ma to dinner Thanksgiving. No fowl—just Pigs in the corn!—little pork sausages baked in corn. They seem to like it at my house [ ]—the windows, I guess, here's where you get light anyhow.

A woman in Fort threw herself into the river off the bridge one night last week. "She must have been insane," they said—you can't help but feel it must have been a lucid moment among patches of ice.

Was going to stay up Friday and go to the Schumann movie but it snowed so much I didn't. At home I felt if only I could read something I had once written, some prose... so I dug around and found the letter that you have re. visit to Kumlien's old homeplace (I made a copy of the letter to remember the place.) Where I am and who I am... everything else is so silly. In the midst of that ordeal two weeks ago I said to myself when I came home and saw a picture of the sora rail, "Only two or three things make the world, one of them you, sora... and those things must be made known...To you, sora...to you [Robert] Burns...to you, silence...child..."

— from a letter to Zukofsky, 1947

26

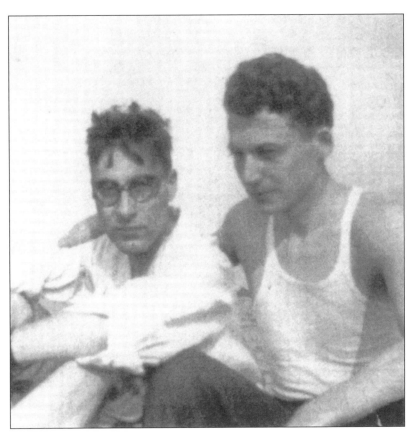

Louis Zukofsky and Jerry Reisman visit Lorine in Wisconsin, 1936.

Chapter Two

And Town Changed Us Too

———

Club 26

Our talk, our books
riled the shore like bullheads
at the roots of the luscious
large water lily

Then we entered the lily
built white on a red carpet

the circular quiet
cool bar

glass stems to caress
We stayed till the stamens trembled

———

LORINE SET HER SIGHTS beyond Blackhawk Island, and her connection to that world beyond was Louis Zukofsky.

[ ] I wish now that suddenly my job would be taken away and I had to write prose for a living, that somebody would say, here, and I had to write on this subject. Maybe I get that way, too, from reading about Thackeray who is an example of a writer working from hand to mouth —chapter by chapter for magazines, often getting them done just in time for the next issue…

On his lecture tour in America as he was riding a train, a newsboy called out "Thackeray's works" so he read A Shabby Genteel Story *for the first time in 12 years. In New York he found oysters served (whole) American style. He hesitated with his fork while his friends urged him on. He took a large specimen and put it back. "It looks just like the High Priest's servant's ear that Peter cut off." He chose the smallest one, downed it in one gulp. They asked him how he felt. He said, "as if I'd swallowed a baby."*

— from a letter to Zukofsky, 1947

Jenny Penberthy, a Niedecker scholar, notes:

"The friendship between Lorine Niedecker and Louis Zukofsky has long perplexed friends and family, readers and critics. Their literary bond is as puzzling as the personal. Where is the common ground between these two poets of such discrepant output and personality? What place in the lofty orbit of Zukofsky studies does Niedecker occupy? How can one account for their forty years' exchange of regular letters, often more than one a week — a correspondence that was for each of them, their greatest production?

"One obstacle to an accurate description of the relationship is that Zukofsky and Niedecker kept it deliberately vague... Over the years of their entire relationship, they destroyed a great number of their accumulated letters, leaving only those that reflect good-humored companionship. Aside from a handful of endearments, the intimacies and the distress of the 1930s are now almost entirely undocumented. After those years, they met no more than half a dozen times but they maintained a steadfast exchange of poetry and letters...

"One of the strongest impressions from both sides of the remaining correspondence is of suppressed information. Parts of the letters, for example, have been censored—words and phrases are heavily scored out or removed altogether. Both poets evidently expected their personal papers to be read and hence put considerable effort into trimming and shaping their voluminous correspondence. Many of the original letters themselves already exercise great tact. They are full of obliquities, juxtapositions, ellipses and the pervasive empty brackets sign [ ]—a signal of deep caring for which words dare not and need not be found. Originally Zukofsky's sign, it came to be used routinely by both. In some of his letters, the sign replaces the more conventional address, 'Dear Lorine.' In others it concludes the letter with what he called a parenthesis full of love. Teasing the limits of confidentiality was evidently another of their games.

"During the period of his son Paul's childhood, Zukofsky's letters are full of accounts of Paul's charming antics and observations. These letters became the source of the poems *For Paul* in two senses: they gave her not only an engaging subject but a written text to quote from, to allude to and to paraphrase. The poems are written in open homage to Paul, but they also bear an embedded homage to Zukofsky... Niedecker's *For Paul* poems delineate a 'family' composed of the Zukofskys, herself and her parents. At first, Celia and Louis welcomed her attachment to Paul, and the child apparently enjoyed her attentions too... Relations had changed during the *For Paul* years. Niedecker's choice of Paul as a focus for her poems had seemed, for a while, to establish a place for her within the Zukofsky household. But something went awry; the poems pressed too far into Zukofsky privacies; perhaps they began to seem too public and intrusive and Zukofsky felt compelled to retreat from the project. In 1961, when two of the poems were to be published in *My Friend Tree*, he asked that she remove the overt biographical content from the titles or dedications."

— from Jenny Penberthy's introduction to *Niedecker and the Correspondence with Zukofsky 1931-1970* (most of what is now published is Lorine Niedecker's side of the correspondence)

———

FOR PAUL

Paul
now six years old:
this book of birds I loved
I give to you.
I thought now maybe Paul
growing taller than cattails
around Duck Pond
between the river and the Sound
will keep this book intact,
fly back to it each summer

maybe Paul

———

———

Your erudition
the elegant flower
of which

my blue chicory
at scrub end
of campus ditch

illuminates

———

March

Bird feeder's
    snow-cap
        sliding
            off

———

Fog-thick morning—
I see only
where I now walk. I carry
    my clarity
with me.

———

Their early relationship explains some of the complexity and con-tradictions of the interaction between Lorine Niedecker and Louis Zukofsky. These are the words of Zukofsky's friend who came to know Lorine well.

"In the early 1930s I lived in the South Bronx with my parents and was a physics major at CCNY. Louis Zukofsky and I were close friends. Frequently, on weekends, I rode the subway to his Manhattan apartment and did my homework there.

"I had read most, if not all, of his letters to and from Lorine

Niedecker. Neither Louis nor I had ever met her and we both looked forward to her impending visit. I believe Louis expected her to stay, at most, two weeks. The year was 1933.

"When Lorine arrived, she and Louis exchanged shy greetings and Louis introduced her to me. Of course she already knew about me from Louis's letters. Later, when she began to unpack her things and Louis saw what she had brought — an ironing board and an iron, for example — he concluded that she was prepared to stay a long time. He looked a bit worried. He had not planned to have a long-term live-in relationship with Lorine.

"I think she, on the other hand, had been in love with Louis ever since she first became acquainted with his work — before she came to New York — and would have been happy to stay with him for life.

"After all these years I can remember some highlights but few details of my friendship with Lorine. This brief account includes almost everything that I can recall.

"Louis's apartment consisted of one room, about halfway below street level. There were two windows on the street side and on the opposite side were a bathroom, a clothes closet and a small table. A bed was located on the left side of the room (looking in through the windows). A weekend visitor would have been likely to find me doing my homework on a folding card table in the center of the room, Louis working at his desk in a corner near one of the windows and Lorine working at the table under the light from a table lamp. Sometimes we'd work for hours in deep silence. Once, Lorine's pen was scratchy and Louis suddenly screamed at her to stop the noise. Lorine was frightened and hurt by his outburst.

"Lorine and Louis visited Louis's friends and received visits from them. I think Lorine met René Taupin, W.C. Williams, George and Mary Oppen, and some of my cousins who were part of our social life. Lorine was taken to movies, art exhibits and museums. On weekends I went along. We walked and talked.

"Louis had received birth-control instructions from Dr. Williams, but apparently there was a misunderstanding somewhere. Williams claimed that his instructions were not carried out completely. Lorine had become pregnant.

"Lorine wanted to keep the child, but Louis insisted that she terminate the pregnancy. Lorine promised to have the child in Wisconsin, raise it on Blackhawk Island and never bother Louis for support money or anything else. Louis was adamant. Nothing remained but to find a reliable abortionist and the money to pay for the operation.

"One of my cousins recommended a fine female doctor. Her fee was $150 — a lot of money in those days. Lorine obtained the money from her father.

"After the operation, the doctor revealed that her patient had been carrying twins. Lorine ruefully named them 'Lost' and 'Found.' Physically, she recovered quickly; but I think she must have ached for her twins all the years of her life.

"Lorine and I had become such close friends by now that Louis urged us to become intimate. We needed no further encouragement.

"I can't remember whether I read Lorine's plays during her visit or whether she sent them to us later; but I do recall that they made a strong impression on me. In those days I was deeply interested in screen writing and I saw her plays not as written for the stage, but rather as movie scenarios without camera instructions. To show her what I meant I added camera instructions to her play *Domestic and Unavoidable*, transforming it into a movie scenario without changing a word of the play. She was very amused, and Louis sent the scenario to Ezra Pound in February 1935 along with the first half of my scenario of Joyce's *Ulysses*.

"Lorine was shy and unworldly, but she was lively and talkative when with people she liked. Her sense of humor sparkled in conversation as it does in her poetry and sometimes she was surprisingly uninhibited. She almost worshipped Louis, who was a phenomenal teacher, by far the best I ever knew, and Lorine was eager to learn. They both recognized each other's literary worth and uniqueness very early in their careers.

"In September 1936 Louis and I visited Lorine on Blackhawk Island and there I began to understand Lorine's home background in greater depth.

"Her mother, whom Lorine had always referred to as 'BP' (Bean Pole) was quite deaf as I recall, religious and straight-laced. She was very upset with Lorine for 'living in sin' with Louis and felt uneasy in Louis's presence. However, she treated me like a son and went out of her way to make me comfortable. I was twenty-two years old, a decade younger than Louis and Lorine and I suppose I aroused maternal instincts in her. Mercifully, I don't think she ever suspected that Lorine was having a relationship with both of her visitors.

"Lorine avoided her mother as much as possible because of the tension between them which apparently had existed for years. Lorine lived in a separate cabin perhaps 100 yards or more away from the main house.

"Lorine's father, Henry, was a dapper man of about fifty. He owned considerable property on the island and made a living providing accommodations for fishermen and hunters. Warm and friendly, he liked to talk about national and world politics and he let me have two of his guns for target practice.

"Henry had a mistress who lived nearby with her husband and a daughter who was probably around eighteen or nineteen years old. The husband knew about his wife's affair, but Henry bought his acquiescence with gifts of land. Lorine worried about the arrangement because she (correctly) foresaw the day when Henry would become landless and poor himself and have nothing to leave her when he died. I was sure Lorine's mother had bitter knowledge of what was going on.

"I was amazed at the soap-opera situation in which Lorine lived and worked. In New York I was impressed with Lorine's courageous wish to return home from her visit, willing to confront her stern mother and a very conservative community with the fact that she was pregnant and unmarried. Now I felt that if she had done so, it would have been just another development in an ongoing drama.

"Frank Heineman, a former student of Louis's at the University of Wisconsin, drove up to Blackhawk Island from Chicago in a rented Ford. He was my age and, like me, had been a physics major. I had met him several times in New York. The four of us had a great time driving around like crazy, rowing on the lake, etc. I remember being in a barn, Frank and I repeatedly climbing up to the rafters, leaping onto a haystack and sliding to the ground while Louis and Lorine watched.

"Henry introduced me to the daughter of his mistress — a very attractive girl. I remember that Lorine didn't like her or her parents. Years later, I heard that she had become a bargirl. Around 1944, when I was living in Towson, Maryland, she wrote to me and asked if she could be my live-in housekeeper. Not long after, I heard that she had been murdered. I must have heard this from Lorine through Louis. However, Glenna Breslin, who recently made visits to

Blackhawk Island and talked to the residents, was told that the girl had died of natural causes.

"When I ended my friendship with Louis in 1947, the most distressing consequence was that I lost contact with Lorine. At this point there was no way that Lorine could have remained friends with both Louis and me. I still miss her."

— Jerry Reisman, 1991

———

"Who was Mary Shelley? / What was her name / before she married?… // Who was Mary Shelley? / She read Greek, Italian / She bore a child // Who died / and yet another child / who died."

— from a Niedecker poem about Mary Shelley

———

My mother saw the green tree toad
on the window sill
her first one
since she was young.
We saw it breathe
and swell up round.
My youth is no sure sign
I'll find this kind of thing
tho it does sing.
Let's take it in

I said so grandmother can see
but she could not
it changed to brown
and town
changed us, too.

———

Each spring flood waters engulfed her little house.

Chapter Three

The Influence of Inference

MORE THAN EVER her letters and her poems were full of the place where Lorine lived.

Wish I had a couple weeks more at home. But I made the best of it. A little marshy, soggy piece west of the house that one could almost call the primordial swamp... I cut grass there and planted willows, my eyes to the green ground so much that I can almost feel sea-water in my veins... little things like algae, fine-haired weeds mixed with large-blade grass, and I think: Equisetum—little fern-like plants with hollow stems—imagine that!—if equisetum is its name—like the guy that found out he had spoken prose all his life. Lots of wild mint where I wanted to mow (with corn knife) but I wouldn't, such sweet little things. Every time I go down there with the intention of mowing I come back without doing it—and I guess my little willows will grow anyhow. I took a walk down a long path beside tall willows out to where the hunters get into their boats for Mud Lake—thousands of willows shoulder high with reddish leaves toward the tops — simply pulled 'em out by the roots and lugged 'em home for my own beginning of creation. I worked all yesterday at this and walked miles within a short space. BP went with me on one jaunt. We saw wild sweet peas (bluish purple and much smaller than tame ones) entwined around the tall grasses, the coolest, freshest looking thing. Yes, June is a good month for you to come some day. Diddly's [Paul's] fireflies too. I am rereading Peattie [an American naturalist]—remember some notes I sent you once?—latest research, he says, shows that bacteria on the firefly cause the light? Luminous bacteria. Symbiotic relationship. Probably the light is not for sexual advantage at all. More like the luminous fungi that sometimes grow on trees. The bacteria on fireflies may not be necessary to the latter's existence, but do them no harm. Continuing with Peattie —"Good poetry is swift-winged, essential and truthful description—and so is good science." Suzzle.

I discovered something—Henry uses trees so much of the time, to mark boundary lines. So I ask: To whom do they belong? So he says: Well, I don't know—who cares?—what do you want to do with trees anyway—they'll always stand. Maybe, it's the beginning of socialization!

— from a letter to Zukofsky, 1948

His voice in me, the river's turn that finds the
Grace in you, four notes first too full for talk, leaf
Lighting stem, stems bound to the branch that binds the
Tree, and then as from the same root we talk, leaf
After leaf of your mind's music, page, walk leaf
Over leaf of his thought, sounding
His happiness: song sounding
The grace that comes from knowing
Things, her love our own showing
Her love in all her honor.

> — the final stanza of Zukofsky's *A-11*

—————

Paul
        when the leaves
                fall

from their stems
        that lie thick
                on the walk

in the light
        of the full note
                the moon
playing
        to leaves
                when they leave

the little
        thin things
                Paul

—————

A winter evening in Wisconsin — I arrived home against a 50 mile icy west wind with a scarf tied over my face to find my oil barrel almost dry (the next day was the day for the oilman to come) and my cistern pump, in the kitchen frozen. I looked in my drinking water pail and hardly a drop there so I turned around and went to the folks with two pails, one for soft water and one for hard. Coming back the water splashed out and it was like standing up on the deck of a ship in a storm. My house was 46 and I turned up the heat. I went out to tip the barrel and turn on the faucet and hold the oil can under it all three things with two hands in the wind and squeezed enough oil for the night. Supper was partaken with boots and scarf on. When it got up to 60 in the house with a wave of air pulsing through from the three west windows I started to clean house in the one little room where I keep my clothes. I kept warm working. About ten o'clock I got through and decided to eat a dish of baked beans and catsup — cap on the catsup bottle wouldn't come off no matter how much I tapped and turned. Crawled into bed, practically under it, said good-bye to the world about eleven. But Saturday spring came and flies on the window. Doesn't look like we'll have high water this spring, thank God for that. A week in a dingy hotel room with all that expense would plunge me into the depths. I remember 3 years ago or was it 4 — I went to hotel and wrote you — will there be a war with Russia?

— from a letter to Zukofsky, 1950

———

Popcorn-can cover
screwed to the wall
over a hole
   so the cold
can't mouse in

———

Springtime's wide
water-
     yield
but the field
will return

———

41

```
       ———

    July, waxwings
    on the berries
    have dyed red
                  the dead
    branch

       ———
```

The flood is subsiding and maybe the monsoon has passed. The birds and animals came close, practically inside the house because on two sides I had only a couple of feet of land. A flood in the summer here is like a tropical jungle. The Amazon flowed through just in front of my thick growth of dogwood. Here a large (very fat) muskrat swam — they seem to swim with their noses as that's what you notice first — and came out in shore to sun himself. What's more wet looking when it's wet than a rat? My family of king rails worked for food, whacking at little crab-like things sailing along but rails are really very shy. Once a rabbit and a rail were eating away both absorbed, looking down — suddenly they came face to face and both jumped back. Rabbits not having bills are quite peaceful creatures — and always nibbling — it's wonder there's any grass left in this world. I seem to have planted my gladioli for them. Living in the teeming tropics under jungle law I wasn't surprised one morning to find two blood spots on my cement steps and not far away a decapitated young rabbit. I had turtles too of course in my mud flat — I can't be sure of the difference between their noises and bull frogs' but I think it's turtles that have that deep thing, always three times, from evening to two in the morning. I'd wake up in my sleep and wonder what all those dogs were doing barking around my house. One day there was a water spaniel plowing through — I soon got him out of there with my cannon like voice and much clapping of hands (bring'em-back-alive-Niedecker) as every time a dog gets excited over a bird and jumps on the soft lawn he leaves a hole. Carp worked on the edge of the lawn and slapped the water in the night. Lots of snakes of course, one disporting himself on a young willow like Spanish moss. I notice frogs get eaten in quantities by almost every-thing. Mozart's Air and Chopin much too delicate for this country but beautiful moonlight nights.

— from a letter to Zukofsky, 1950

My Life by Water

My life
   by water —
      Hear

spring's
   first frog
      or board

out on the cold
   ground
      giving

Muskrats
   gnawing
      doors

to wild green
   arts and letters
      Rabbits

raided
   my lettuce
      One boat

two —
   pointed toward
      my shore

thru birdstart
   wingdrip
      weed-drift

of the soft
   and serious —
      Water

Lorine Niedecker's poetry, so simple at first glance, is multi-layered, demanding that the reader mine beneath the surface for its riches as the critic Rachel Blau DuPlessis does.

"With Niedecker, haiku seems to have been a means to commentary so buried, so deeply imbedded in apparently artless word choice, line break and tone that the resonances are very delayed. With Niedecker's work in haiku, one must tune in to a very subtle form of closure, one which sometimes leaves one questioning her adequacy at managing rhetoric, but eventually asks you to question your own need for fullness, plentitude, plethora and glut. The facade of inability, artlessness and the almost unspoken hint are very feminine strategies; her haiku furthermore work as gifts on a small personal scale. Haiku are part of a poetic exchange which she constructed with both Zukofsky and Corman. Working on this personal scale, one makes a familial economy of sharing which rejects the feedback loop of impersonal publication, prize-winning poetry and fame. She wrote to Charles Reznikoff, 'Reading *Inscriptions: 1944–56*, I often feel a kinship between us in the short poem. And if you are my brother-in-poetry then we have Chinese and Japanese brothers. But I have a great deal of practicing to do —of quiet insight—before I can enter such a good family.' In addition, from a class perspective, the lack of high poetic language (in Anglophone haiku) infuses dailiness and life as it is lived with the possibility of poetry.

"*My Life by Water* draws upon the radical condensations of haiku; this work may be thought of as an elaboration of the 'sound of water / water sound' of Basho's great haiku about the frog jumping into the pond. And as 'watersound,' the word 'by' in the title might mean next to — as Niedecker spent her life in the flood-prone spillway, 'a section of low land on the Rock River where it empties into Lake Koshkonong.' But 'by' might at the same time open the much-debated questions of authorship and point of view. Could this really be the 'life' of someone, her biography, whose author is water? The Keats epitaph is suggested: 'Here lies one whose name was writ BY water.' Her self is put in the doubled position of water and author. Water surrounds her as amniotic medium and author of herself; she writes the 'water borne' or water-related aspects of her life. The fluidity of boundary between self and setting is a theme: she sees boats 'pointed toward / my shore,' or may herself be the 'one boat' which 'two' (her parents) 'pointed' there.

"Nine intensely compressed three-line stanzas are framed by two dashes, so the whole poem is caught (dammed) between the word 'My life / by water' and 'Water.' She catalogues animals: frogs, muskrats and rabbits, whose activities are in some continuum with human and other forms inhabiting the same terrain. Either a frog's 'ribbit' or a cold board makes a cracking noise. Muskrats create 'wild green / arts and letters,' a diploma of nature, from, or out of the 'doors,' that separate us from the out-of-doors. The 'lettuce' nibbled by the rabbits chimes pointedly with our phrase for the humanities as a discipline: letters / lettuce.

"The little stanzas climax in a series of kenning-like combinations. The words birdstart or wingdrip remove the transparency and limpidity of nature; the compound neologisms are a thrust of linguistic possession without possessiveness, that ebbs in the loosening of the hyphenated 'weed-drift.' She is mothered by, nourished by the place. Niedecker need not search for anything beyond the 'here' in which (and much is through the ear in her work) one can 'hear.' With the ear, she tempers the domination of the 'eye' and scopic practices. With the descriptions, she features intersubjectivity and a webbing of relations. The poet sustains an attitude of wonder and readiness at the quirky holiness of the ordinary. The universe is non-dualistic — both awkward and beautiful.

"If this poem is autobiography, it is also her poetic: a poetic of rumination, meditation, circling around and 'reflection.' 'The basis is direct and clear—what has been seen or heard—but,' stated Niedecker, 'something gets in, overlays all that to make a state of consciousness.' There is an 'awareness of everything influencing everything' with networks of linkages and not the 'hard, clear image' only. But this is a poem which also tracks a political attitude: how to have the environment as a source without imposing ownership. Possessions (as things, pots, clothes, appliances) and possession (as mediumship, shamanistic behaviors, poetic transcendence, vatic or bardic claims) are both forcefully put on notice in Niedecker's work."

— from *Lorine Niedecker, The Anonymous: Gender, Class, Genre and Resistances* by Rachel Blau DuPlessis

———

You see here
the influence
of inference

Moon on rippled
stream

"Except as
and unless"

———

*Much taken up with how to define a way of writing poetry which is not
Imagist nor Objectivist fundamentally nor Surrealism alone — Stella
Leonardos of Brazil senses something when I loosely called it "reflections"
or as I think it over now, reflective, maybe. The basis is direct and clear
— what has been seen or heard, etc...— but something gets in, overlays
all that to make a state of consciousness... The visual form is there in the
background, and the words convey what the visual form gives off after
it's felt in the mind. A heat that is generated and takes in the whole world
of the poem. A light, a motion, inherent in the whole. Not surprising,
since modern poetry and old poetry, if it's good, proceeds not from one
point to the next linearly but in a circle. The tone of the thing. And
awareness of everything influencing everything. Early in life I looked
back of our buildings to the lake and said, "I am what I am because of all
this — I am what is around me — those woods have made me..." I used
to feel that I was goofing off unless I held only to the hard, clear image,
the thing you could put your hand on, but now I dare do this reflection.
For instance,* Origin *will have a narrow, longish poem, sensuous, begins,
"My life / in water" and ends, "of the soft / and serious — / Water"...*

—from a letter to Gail Roub, 1967

Henry, Lorine (age ten) and Daisy, July 1913.

Chapter Four

At the Close — Someone

"A poem is a peculiar instance of language's uses, and goes well beyond the [person] writing — finally to the anonymity of any song."
— from *Collected Essays of Robert Creeley*

BP died last Wednesday and was buried Saturday. [ ] She never got to the mental ward, the Jefferson Hospital is a regular hospital in connection with the county home for old people and mental defectives. I suppose it must have been apparent that her wandering was the result of morphine, digitalis which is a poison, and the natural toxin in her body. It was always amazing how clear she was, at that! You'd think she'd be sleeping and when Henry would pull out his watch to see if visiting hours were almost over, she'd say, "Now don't sneak out." One day she said in a frantic moment, "Don't omit these visits up here." Her last words may not have been of importance, she sat up for her supper an hour after we left and then fell back dead. But her last words to me were, "Wash the floors, wash the clothes and pull weeds."
— from a letter to Zukofsky, 1951

Strings of geese going over—thunder in the distance and spiders starting to crawl. — from a letter to Zukofsky, 1955

———

Old Mother turns blue and from us
   "Don't let my head drop to the earth.
I'm blind and deaf." Death from the heart,
   a thimble in her purse.

"It's a long day since last night.
   Give me space. I need
floors. Wash the floors, Lorine! —
   wash clothes! Weed!"

———

I like the Robert Creeley poems you sent me — I'd be writing something like that if I weren't so form conscious — a heightened prose with a rather large rhythm, a slightly mystic, abstract way of getting reality across. I have to be more concentrated, tho I am beginning to worry about the five-line haiku-derived form that dogs me now, it doesn't fit everything. Maybe I am not object-minded enough, not minutely eye-seeing enough to fit a symbolism because you have only a few words to use. When I read your concise, bare but sharp lines, I think both Creeley and I are on the wrong track, the wrong hill, looking out and seeing everything and nothing.

... The business of loneliness — the mind has to be sharp to keep one from getting uselessly involved just for the sake of a moment of less loneliness. I have the Art News Annual, *that large book you get from Marboro Books at one-fourth the cost when it's a year old and I carried it to work one day thinking to ask the record librarian if she'd like to borrow it — she has a daughter in Milwaukee who paints. I didn't approach her, after carrying the thing there! I think they know they have a cleaning woman who is a little different from the usual, but it wouldn't do the slightest good to show them how different.*

— from a letter to Zukofsky, 1958

———

Hear
where her snow-grave is
the *You*
  ah you
of mourning doves

———

How white the gulls
in grey weather
    Soon April
    the little
yellows

———

There's a better shine
on the pendulum
than is on my hair
and many times

•• ••

I've seen it there.

———

If only my friend
would return
and remove the leaves
    from my eaves
troughs

———

I've been away from poetry. Home yesterday. Took a man along to get the tacked carpet and mat up — soaked and gooey and weighing a ton. We threw it all into the water tho carpet could have been dried somewhere and some poor soul might have wanted it. I have no other "loss" except portable clothes closet. Plastic clothes bags that hang from hooks are better anyhow.

For awhile I'll use just wood floor with scatter rugs. Still have linoleum to get up off kitchen and bathroom floors. Left windows open (screens in) and stove burning on low. I'll get along! Next weekend if I can get this man again we'll have it ready to live in again.

First thing we did yesterday was move the heater to get the rug out from under it. The stove pipes fell out but black soot was nothing, having already the mud of the Delta. One time he asked for a broom. I said: "The broom is wet, it stood in it." He: "Naturally it's wet."

The umbrella had stood in it and the stick is so swollen you can't make it catch to stay open.

The runway to the shed in which I keep my power mower lost its moorings at the end and flaps in the waves, still attached to the sill of the shed — this runway is a part of the side of the old General Atkinson, the first large boat (launch) my father had — he bought it 40 years ago.

You can't see a water-line on the mop board nor actually on the table legs and anyway I can re-touch with some kind of polish.

O well, the place still stands!

Harold [a local man she met and hoped to marry] talks of going to California where his brother is a physician, Long Beach, I believe when he retires after five more years of dentistry. He told me that right away at first but I counted on this coming winter when he can't get here too often to become lonely enough to revoke that decision or take me with him. And five years is a long time anyhow. I suppose I no longer count on his marrying me. All the doors have never been opened to me in my life but closing some of them has let more of something else into a few or into one or two and there'll be poetry and that's that.

Yes and notice the letter from Corman! That word slight again! Tell me what you think he means by too much written, these poems enclosed. I think he means poems by younger writers are more suggestive by not being wordy e.g. Samperi's. What do you think? I notice Corman says slight but then says they're weighted! I do have to work to become more concentrated, sharper and yet further removed as in pure imagination. I can't phone him or see him of course while he's in Chicago. Don't have anything else on hand that isn't already printed.

— from a letter to Zukofsky, 1960

———

I've been away from poetry
many months

and now I must rake leaves
with nothing blowing

between your house
and mine

———

―――

EASTER

A robin stood by my porch
and side-eyed
raised up
a worm

―――

Get a load
of April's
fabulous

frog rattle —
lowland freight cars
in the night

―――

*For me the sentence lies in wait — all those prepositions and connectives
— like an early spring flood. A good thing my follow-up feeling has
always been condense, condense.*

— from a letter to Cid Corman, 1962

*Water on running board of pick-up truck as we ride to work. Pussy
willows big, their tops above water. Whistling swans here but also as yet
ice on both lakes. Get up at 5:00, leave home at 6:15, home at 5:00 —
O but poems floating in.*

— from a letter to Zukofsky, 1962

Her parents both dead, Lorine finds solace with a man who in some
outward characteristics resembles her father.

*The first time Al Millen came (about the house — wanted to buy it, the
one in trouble) I thought: if this relationship grows it would be something
like Lady Chatterley's lover. By this time, I see there's more and more actu-
ally in common between us — he really reads, knows who I mean by
Voltaire, Bertrand Russell, likes H.G. Wells's fiction, knows who Robert
Frost was (when I tried to tell him what meant so much to me, poetry). But
all this is nothing — he is even more gentle and tender than Harold — seems
near to tears at times, like my father often seemed. And he has a lovely,*

In 1963 Lorine married Al Millen.

lovely humor. I know this is it. What an adjustment for me—too bad for me to become used to daily companionship, to deep affection, to human(!) happiness. I fear it, upsetting to the other thing I've built up in me that, give me another couple of years, would withstand the world, would never need any other life but itself and things like money, peoples' follies and hatreds and all the silly coming and going wouldn't even be there.

What—what—what? I'll marry him. Somehow I'll work it out, time and space for poetry.

If you get a March Poetry *I'll be happy for it for my birthday—if you don't get one, I'll buy it.*

— from a letter to Zukofsky, 1963

——

I married

in the world's black night
for warmth
      if not repose
      At the close—
someone.

I hid with him
from the long range guns.
      We lay leg
      in the cupboard, head
in closet.

A slit of light
at no bird dawn—
      Untaught
      I thought
he drank

too much.
I say
      I married
      and lived unburied.
I thought—

——

The frog book by Shimpei Kusano [which Corman translated] so very nice, so frog-green. The periods [dots] are the frogs singing silently.

We have frogs here now and sora rails giggling. No flood this spring, very unnatural.

Unnatural, also my immanent [sic] marriage. At sixty, one does foolish things. I hope I'm happy! He's my connection with life.

Till life settles down, this frog is singing silently.

I want to send money after a bit. These books can't come out without cost.

— from a letter to Corman, 1963

———

I knew a clean man
but he was not for me.
Now I sew green aprons
over covered seats. He

wades the muddy water fishing,
falls in, dries his last pay-check
in the sun, smooths it out
in *Leaves of Grass*. He's
the one for me.

———

"They were an odd couple. He possessed a gruff humor; she was clumsy in many things, but not her art. Her literary friends did not know what to make of her unpolished husband. His grown children from a former marriage didn't know what to make of this little woman with thick glasses who, as her husband said, 'scribbled' all the time.

"In 1963, her sixtieth year, Lorine Faith Niedecker was living alone in a one-and-one-half-room cabin on the north shore of the Rock River near where it flows into Lake Koshkonong, three miles west of Fort Atkinson. Her eyesight failing, her parents long dead, she supported herself by scrubbing floors at night at Fort Atkinson Memorial Hospital.

"In 1963, Albert O. Millen, then in his fifty-ninth year, was living alone in a two-room, walk-up apartment in the back of a remodeled duplex at 2042 S. 6th Street, within sight of Saint Josaphat Basilica on Milwaukee's South Side.

"A hard drinker, he and Margaret, his wife of twenty-nine years, had divorced more or less peacefully in 1957, after the youngest of their four children, Gael, graduated from Pulaski High School and left for college.

"Millen had grown up in a hamlet in Northeastern Minnesota. He had lost his left hand in a printing press accident in Oshkosh in his 20s, and now he was a maintenance painter working the third shift for the Ladish Company in Cudahy.

"With a retirement of fishing in mind, Millen bought a grey cottage from Niedecker, a few lots east of Niedecker's cabin. That is how Al and Lorine met. She had inherited several properties from her late parents, Henry and Theresa Niedecker, Henry, a carp seiner and philanderer, Theresa, or Daisy, a stone-deaf, bitter recluse.

"Lorine married a local man in 1928. Although they had separated for good by 1930 she did not file for divorce until 1942. Except for two years as a student at Beloit College and four years working in Madison ending in 1942, she lived on Blackhawk Island, for years tending her invalid mother, for many more years alone in her cabin. Until 1961, when plumbing was installed, she lived without running water or indoor toilet.

"From her marriage onward, she had two roles. As poet, she lived mostly through correspondence. Occasionally literary friends would come to Milwaukee, Madison or Fort Atkinson to visit her and, in usually awkward incidents, sometimes would meet Al. Her other role was as Mrs. Al Millen. She quit her hospital job. He taught her cooking; they took long driving vacations north and west. For the first time as an adult she had modest financial security. They visited Al's children and his grandchildren at their homes; the children visited Blackhawk Island. What is more, in the next seven years, Niedecker increased her output of poetry.

"'Why did this woman who was so sensitive and so involved in her world out there, and seemingly happy with it, why did she marry this man who was so seemingly different from her?' Gail Roub asked in beginning a story he had told before.

"In 1963 or 1964, Gail Roub met Lorine Niedecker, whom he'd often seen walking along the road. In 1964, she would have been sixty-one, he thirty-eight. It was the beginning of an important friendship. At least two Niedecker poems directly relate to Roub, one inspired by a Roub painting, the other by the birth of Gail and Bonnie Roub's first child.

"Roub said: 'I know a little about it. Nobody ever knows the whole story between a husband and wife, a man and a woman, but I sense it was an uneasy marriage. I sensed that he didn't think too much of me. Of course, I was unmarried at the time. I represented some kind of threat to him. I could talk to her a little bit about the poetry and things of the mind, and all that, whereas I don't think he understood the poetry at all...'

"One day Roub invited Lorine to see his slides of Europe, but she was reluctant.

"'I said, "And bring Al along, too." She said, "He wouldn't want to do that." I said, "Well, then you come and see them."

"'I had a friend who used to tie up his boat at my place there, and he was over one night and so I set up that she would come when he was there...

"'Well, she came. She was uneasy, more than I'd ever seen her be uneasy... She stayed maybe for half an hour and she got up and said, "I have to go."

"'I said, "Well, there are more to see." She said, "I have to go. I have to get back home." I said, "We'll walk you home."

"'So we did, we walked her back to the house and as (my friend) and I walked her to the door there, out came Al Millen and said, "What the hell is going on here?" He was really angry, you know. I don't know if he had been drinking. He did have a drinking problem...

"'We backed out very quickly, out back down the road... Then we got back to my house here and the phone rang, and it was Lorine saying, "He's left here. He's coming that way and he's got a gun. Turn off the lights and lock the doors."

"'Well, he did come. He walked up on the porch and pounded on the door and not a sound from within, you know. And eventually he went away, and that was the end of it and I never heard any more from him about it.

"'Then, later, after I married and after I had done some things to get control of the river level out there, which was always a problem... he grudgingly said to Lorine, "Well, maybe Gail isn't so bad after all."

"'After that, he was fairly friendly to me, but I never felt easy around him.

"'When that incident happened, we talked together on the phone, and she said, "You know he got drunk the night we were married." I said, "Oh, that's terrible, Lorine." She said, "He offered, though, to divorce me the next day," and I said, "You should have accepted."

"'She said, "Well, Gail, it isn't so bad. You know, he's the only man who ever told me he loved me."'

— from the essay, *"At the Close—Someone": Lorine's Marriage To Al Millen* by Paul G. Hayes

———

Alcoholic dream
that ran him
   out from home
      to return
leaning

like the house
in this old part
   of town leaves him
  grieving:
why

do I hurt you
whom I love?
  Your ear
    is cold!—here
drink

———

59

———

Wilderness

You are the man
You are my other country
and I find it hard going

You are the prickly pear
You are the sudden violent storm

the torrent to raise the river
to float the wounded doe

———

Lorine Niedecker on Blackhawk Island, 1967.

Chapter Five

A Pencil for a Wing Bone

———

Fall

We must pull
the curtains—
we haven't any
leaves

———

JUST AS LORINE NIEDECKER BELIEVED poetry proceeds not from one point to the next, linearly, but in a circle, her life, too, seems circular and full of parallels. Her love of poetry led to a correspondence with Louis Zukofsky, a brief affair, an abortion, her return to menial jobs in Wisconsin and an intense interest in Louis's son. As we've seen this obsession resulted in the series of poems, *For Paul*, which earned her some of her first critical acclaim. And in her poetry as in her life, there is always the presence of her beloved Rock River — isolating, overflowing, life-giving and ultimately reassuring in its cycle through repeated seasons.

We now join Lorine toward the end of her life. As she gains recognition, Zukofsky turns against her. But with her release from his grip, her writing gains new intensity and she produces what many believe to be her greatest work, *Paean to Place*.

I think both LZ's and my last years are going to be very selfish ones. We've reached an age — 8 years (with me) to 70. It would be nice to imbibe from whatever source we can something of that silence that you, still young, already have. Not that I'm doddering, or as sick as Z. Silence I mean in which to write our poetry.
—from a letter to Corman, 1965

"Relations between Zukofsky and Niedecker changed in the mid-1960s as he began to withdraw from many of his former friends. She became more and more afraid of offending his propriety... By the end of 1965, sensitivity became complete withdrawal, precipitated by her hope to publish a selection of the letters he had written to her over the years. After varied compositional exercises in quotation from letters (both within poems and as the basis for entire poems) here was an opportunity to select passages from a body of letters to which only she had access, and to select them as she would for a poem, so as to express the essence of the mind behind them. This would be her most complete tribute to Zukofsky."

— from Jenny Penberthy's introduction to *Niedecker
and the Correspondence with Zukofsky 1931-1970*

———

CITY TALK (Part II)

I'm good for people? —
penetrating? — if you mean

I'm rotting here —
I'm an alewife

the fish the seagull
has no taste for

I die along the shore
and send a bad smell in

———

————

*I visit
the graves*

Great grandfather
under wild flowers sons
sons here now I
          eye
of us all

but sonless
see no

          hop
clover boy to stop
before me

————

My friend tree
I sawed you down
but I must attend
an older friend
the sun

————

I've started editing the letters LZ has sent me over a 30 year period. It's a chore tho I wouldn't want him to know that. He thinks my time could be well used otherwise — doing my own poems — but he's given me permission. And I see something there — Cid, I wonder if it's ever been done, just the essence, tincture of Z!, a drop to a page, that constant, deep-in spot in his being. It will not be letters in the ordinary sense and of course long ago I destroyed the parts of the letters that he wouldn't want the public to see — oh things that were sharp and brought out the full flavor of LZ, however. But I've always abided by what he's asked.

— from a letter to Corman, 1965

———

Something in the water
like a flower
will devour

water

flower

———

"Niedecker sent Zukofsky a 370-page typescript hoping that once he'd approved it, she could select ten to twenty pages for the *Paris Review* and some for Corman's *Origin*. On October 7, 1965, she wrote to Corman: 'Does LZ agree to your plan for that summer issue? In letters to me he is not very eager to see much of it printed and not at all sure he wants to spend any time on it — cats and *A* come first — yet he demands the carbon I retained here...' There is no further mention of the book so one assumes that Zukofsky did not give her permission to publish it.

"We note Zukofsky's absence from Jonathan Williams's *Epitaphs for Lorine*, which includes tributes from thirty-two poets, among them Cid Corman, Basil Bunting, Ian Hamilton Finlay, Jonathan Williams, Charles Reznikoff, George Oppen, Kenneth Cox and Gael Turnbull."

— from Jenny Penberthy's introduction to *Niedecker and the Correspondence with Zukofsky 1931-1970*

"How upset she was when Zu made waves about the letters, and I seem to remember that she felt something irreparable had happened after she placed the letters at Austin [The University of Texas Humanities Research Center]. It bothered her grievously. I know this is an accurate recollection because it has stayed with me over the years, her unhappiness about all that."

— Gail Roub, 1990

———

The smooth black stone
I picked up in the true source park
    the leaf beside it
once was stone

Why should we hurry
Home

———

I'm sorry to have missed
    Sand Lake
My dear one tells me
    we did not
We watched a gopher there

———

"She was waiting for us at the door, smiling. A plain country woman, very plain, that's what you saw... plain, broad face, plain gingham dress, everything about her cheerful and outgoing, as I knew it so well in the Middle West, optimistic, bouncy, and in her case, bright and hard-edged alert... She was devoid of any affectation or literary manner, which was right down my alley, and I felt immediately comfortable and was all set for a memorable talk, but it didn't happen. We started out all right, chatting about her correspondence with Zukofsky, his comments about the new work she used to send him. Were they complimentary? I asked. 'Oh no!' she cried, 'they were cruel, mean-tempered, sometimes angry.' There was no trace of any resentment or hurt in her voice, however. On the contrary, she laughed and looked fond, as if she were basking in a warm memory. As we talked on, I got an unmistakable sense of something very personal, even physical, in her commitment to Louie. This took a different turn when with a pointed look that seemed to indicate that she assumed that anyone as close to Louie as I, must be highly perceptive and would have to agree with her, it was so obvious, 'Of course,' she remarked, 'you agree, don't you, that Zukofsky is the greatest poet in America.' The look she gave me was probing as well as pointed, so maybe she wasn't altogether sure about me and was testing — or to put the best face on it, just trying to establish a common ground and sympathy to go on. But it had the opposite effect because if there's anything I detest it's the game of rating poets. I can't take hero-worship seriously. In addition, although we had been close friends and I had the utmost confidences in his critical faculties, I didn't feel the same way at all about his short poems, which were all — and I had not read them all — I knew of his work up to that time. Her evaluation, therefore, seemed to me preposterous. 'Oh no!' I replied, as if the idea were slightly amusing. Her face stopped and became serious for a moment, considering this unexpected response, then resumed being friendly, as if nothing had happened. We chatted on for a while but this time only on safe, innocuous subjects. Finally I drifted away and spent the rest of the afternoon with Al. He was puttering round in an outdoor shed which had been converted into a workshop. He was glad to talk and easy to be with. I didn't find him either ordinary or extraordinary, nor did I get any clues that would shed light on this union of perfectionist poet and working man. When Lorine and I parted, it was friendly enough but we both knew we had not become friends and that we would not be seeing each other again."

— from *An Interview with Carl Rakosi*, 1987

PAEAN TO PLACE

And the place
was water

Fish
    fowl
        flood
     Water lily mud
My life

in the leaves and on water
My mother and I
           born
in swale and swamp and sworn
to water

My father
thru marsh fog
    sculled down
        from high ground
saw her face

at the organ
bore the weight of lake water
     and the cold—
he seined for carp to be sold
that their daughter

might go high
on land
    to learn
Saw his wife turn
deaf

and away
She
    who knew boats
       and ropes
no longer played

69

She helped him string out nets
for tarring
    And she could shoot
        He was cool
to the man

who stole his minnows
by night and next day offered
    to sell them back
        He brought in a sack
of dandelion greens

if no flood
No oranges — none at hand
    No marsh marigolds
        where the water rose
He kept us afloat

I mourn her not hearing canvasbacks
their blast-off rise
    from the water
        Not hearing sora
rail's sweet

spoon-tapped waterglass-
descending scale-
    tear-drop-tittle
        Did she giggle
as a girl?

His skiff skimmed
the coiled celery now gone
    from these streams
        due to carp
He knew duckweed

fall-migrates
toward Mud Lake bottom
    Knew what lay
        under leaf decay
and on pickerelweeds

before summer hum
To be counted on:
    new leaves
        new dead
leaves

He could not
—like water bugs—
    stride surface tension
        He netted
loneliness

As to his bright new car
my mother—her house
    next his—averred:
        A hummingbird
can't haul

Anchored here
in the rise and sink
    of life—
        middle years' nights
he sat

beside his shoes
rocking his chair
    Roped not "looped
        in the loop
of her hair"

I grew in green
slide and slant
        of shore and shade
                Child-time—wade
thru weeds

Maples to swing from
Pewee-glissando
        sublime
                slime-
song

Grew riding the river
Books
        at home-pier
                Shelley could steer
as he read

I was the solitary plover
a pencil
        for a wing-bone
From the secret notes
I must tilt

upon the pressure
execute and adjust
        In us sea-air rhythm
"We live by the urgent wave
of the verse"

Seven-year molt
for the solitary bird
        and so young
Seven years the one
dress

for town once a week
One for home
    faded blue-striped
as she piped
her cry

Dancing grounds
my people had none
    woodcocks had—
    backland-
air around

Solemnities
such as what flower
    to take
    to grandfather's grave
unless

water lilies—
he who'd bowed his head
    to grass as he mowed
    Iris now grows
on fill

for the two
and for him
    where they lie
    How much less am I
in the dark than they?

Effort lay in us
before religions
    at pond bottom
    All things move toward
the light

except those
that freely work down
    to oceans' black depths
        In us an impulse tests
the unknown

River rising — flood
Now melt and leave home
    Return — broom wet
        naturally wet
Under
soak-heavy rug
water-bugs hatched —
    no snake in the house
        Where were they? —
she

who knew how to clean up
after floods
    he who bailed boats, houses
        Water endows us
with buckled floors

You with sea water running
in your veins sit down in water
    Expect the long-stemmed blue
        speedwell to renew
itself

O my floating life
Do not save love
    for things
        Throw *things*
to the flood

ruined
by the flood
    Leave the new unbought—
        all one in the end—
water

I possessed
the high word:
    The boy my friend
        played his violin
in the great hall

On this stream
my moonnight memory
    washed of hardships
        maneuvers barges
thru the mouth

of the river
They fished in beauty
    It was not always so
        In Fishes
red Mars

rising
rides the sloughs and sluices
    of my mind
        with the persons
on the edge

———

Chapter Six

To Weep a Deep Trickle

——

Along the river
      wild sunflowers
over my head
      the dead
who gave me life
      give me this
our relative the air
      floods
our rich friend
      silt

——

"My wife and I — on a visit to Fort Atkinson I had promised us for many years — met Lorine and Al on November 15, 1970 (that is, within a few weeks of the stroke that was to claim her life, not poetry, the last day of the year). They had suggested we stay at the Blackhawk Hotel, dowdy, but clean, convenient and reasonable, in the center of the town. It was one day, about eight hours in all we spent together. We had waited for it.

"…I spoke to her from a Fort Atkinson outskirts telephone box, receiving directions to the Blackhawk Hotel. It was about 11 p.m., but she and Al retired at sundown always and she thought it was about 2 – 3 a.m.

"Perhaps some of my journal notes of the visit might fall properly here… My words are candid:

15th Nov (Sunday):
    Up about 8:30. Day partly cloudy/cool and bright… Breakfast (at hotel) about 11:00 and as figured Al and Lorine came in while we were amidst it. Okay. Al a Minnesota back-

woodsman: a guy — with a satisfaction in the manly formula — gentle at heart, but clumsy. Lorine shy and gentle. Bright and true. Incapable of crudity. Lonely/eager for intellectual company but unable to foment it, fearful of the 'larger' scene. Not quite as bold as Emily — but a genuine voice and spirit.

Her preparations didn't altogether come off — but they were not our 'reason' for visiting. Al likes his football games, etc.; he likes the adventurous and vigorous: the quiet and meditative puts him at a disadvantage and doesn't stir him. He's a fair storyteller and has good stories from childhood to tell. He lacks, however, 'realization'—so that the stories can only have whatever depth someone else might draw from them...

Supper was chicken, stuffing, string beans, orange cranberry, cottage cheese and plenty of everything. She will, no doubt, apologize for the meal in her next letter — needlessly. But their tiny place was cozy and good. They don't quite hit it off—but both have been thru enough to give to each other — even when impatient. They could never have mated at an earlier age (he was divorced after twenty-nine years of marriage).

Recorded L. reading newer poems...

Stayed with them — at their riverside place — till about 7:30 or so. (Given coat/jackets against cold.) Then back here (hotel) for a drink at the bar...

"I'll add more detail from memory.

"She made it clear that, but for a younger teacher friend across the river, she had no intellectual companionship in the area, and likely never did have any. Her library was well-stocked and ranging. She showed me photos of her father and herself on the river. Told me some of the history of Black Hawk. Al, one-armed (lost his left arm in a machine as a young man), was readily engrossed in the TV. Its main use for her was that it was a distraction for him. They had ample means for their modest existence.

"Some children came to the door and Lorine instinctively, very gently, addressed them, went to the icebox and gave them some candy bars left over from Halloween, when they had gone, to her dismay, unclaimed. Al boasted of being frightening to them and was not averse to flashing a gun, if they got too noisy. Lorine naturally shied at his style, but didn't press the issue.

"She read poorly, but her eyesight was poor and she was using a magnifying glass to read by and she had never done it before. It was the music on the page that she explored. She read her Jefferson, Morris and Darwin pieces.

"At the hotel bar, Al and I had beers and the ladies had Lorine's favorite 'grasshoppers'...

"Her voice had a brittleness, largely of age, I think; it would've been sweeter altogether in earlier years. Even so, her gentleness and concern came through in the short recording I made of her, fortunately, so soon before her death.

"She was small and slight, but taller than Shizumi — of course. There was an accent betraying a non-urban existence—though Fort Atkinson is not a farming community—nor is the Blackhawk Island region she lived in—right on the water. It almost seems like summer resort country—for those who might like inland fishing—and quiet.

"Her style was neat, unaggressive without being timid or diffident. She knew what she felt and what she wanted, but she would not impose either feeling or desire on others...

"Her poems are often 'literary': that is, related to her reading— but they never are merely intellectual or abstract. You can feel her delight in the experiences of others and especially the language in which experiences have been touched and realized. She has an exquisite ear for detail. Every word is lived. You can feel her in them. She culls them. This is provender.

"She had ample cause to be self-pitying and bitter, but her letters to me show no trace of either qualification. Her complaints, when they occur, and only rarely do they occur, are clearly hard wrung and never in excess of provocation. She is unusually well-balanced in her judgments and perspicacious and particular. She is both unpredictable and characteristic. She has learned from others, but projects her own music and her own realizations. There is no sense of complacency.

"It aches me yet — her absence. When a new book of mine appears I keep wanting to send her a copy—for no one seems ever to have drawn so much from them—though she never was given to flattery or exaggeration. Poetry was her life and her life remains for us as poetry—thanks to her magnanimous gift."

— from Cid Corman's essay,
With Lorine: A Memorial, 1903-1970

———

Now in one year
    a book published
    and plumbing—
took a lifetime
  to weep
      a deep
         trickle

———

"I think of lines of poetry that I might use,
all day long and even in the night."

      — Lorine Niedecker's last recorded words

Lorine Niedecker was buried in Union Cemetery, two and one-half miles from where she lived, during a blizzard on January 3, 1971. Al Millen died in 1981. He was buried next to the Niedecker plot. There are two stones side by side. A large one stands over the graves of three people. It reads:

Neidecker [sic]

Henry	Theresa	Lorine
1879–1954	1878–1951	1903–1970

Under Lorine's name and outside the border, the name "Millen" was etched later. Al's much smaller stone proudly states:

Albert O. Millen
1904–1981
Husband of
Lorine Niedecker

Bibliography

Books by Lorine Niedecker

New Goose (Prairie City, Illinois: Press of James A. Decker, 1946)

My Friend Tree (Edinburgh, Scotland: Wild Hawthorn Press, 1961)

North Central (London, England: Fulcrum Press, 1968)

T & G: The Collected Poems (1936-1966) (Penland, North Carolina: Jargon Society, 1969); enlarged as *My Life by Water: Collected Poems, 1936-1968* (London, England: Fulcum Press, 1970)

Blue Chicory (New Rochelle, New York: Elizabeth Press, 1976)

The Granite Pail: The Selected Poems of Lorine Niedecker, edited by Cid Corman (San Francisco, California: North Point Press, 1985)

From This Condensery: The Complete Writing of Lorine Niedecker, edited by Robert J. Bertholf (East Haven, Connecticut: Jargon Society/Inland Book Company, 1985)

Lorine Niedecker: Collected Works, edited by Jenny Penberthy (Berkeley and Los Agneles, Califronia, London, England: University of California Press, 2002)

Niedecker Letters

"Between Your House and Mine": The Letters of Lorine Niedecker to Cid Corman 1960 to 1970, edited by Lisa Pater Faranda (Durham, North Carolina: Duke University Press, 1986)

Niedecker and the Correspondence with Zukofsky, 1931-1970, edited by Jenny Penberthy (New York, New York: Cambridge University Press, 1993)

Lorine Niedecker: Woman & Poet, edited by Jenny Penberthy (Orono, Maine: National Poetry Foundation, 1996)

Other Books

The Full Note, edited by Peter Dent (Devon, England: Interim Press, 1983)

Lorine Niedecker, An Original Biography, by Jane Shaw Knox (Fort Atkinson, Wisconsin: Dwight Foster Public Library, n.d.)

Lorine Niedecker: The Solitary Plover, by Phyllis Walsh (Richland Center, Wisconsin: Juniper Press, 1992)

Appendix

Touring Blackhawk Island

LORINE NIEDECKER WAS BORN and spent most of her life on Blackhawk Island near Fort Atkinson, Wisconsin. It's a low, marshy peninsula along which the Rock River flows before emptying into Lake Koshkonong, one of Wisconsin's largest lakes. Blackhawk Island Road runs the length of the island. On either side of the road, for about three miles, are cottages and houses. This area has been a haven for hunters and fishermen. Black Hawk, war chief of the Sauk Indians, lived there briefly during the Black Hawk War of 1832.

The vegetation is typical of a flood plain. It contains maple, elm, alder, ash, willow, wild calla, cattails, reeds, rushes and the equisetum mentioned in Lorine's letter. The area attracts many birds — crows, robins, chickadees, grackles, orioles, redwing blackbirds, blue jays, wrens, hawks and even blue herons, egrets, sandhill cranes, Canada geese, swans and rails, notably the sora rail celebrated in several of her poems. It's also inhabited by frogs, turtles, snakes, muskrats, river otters, dragonflies and other insects.

Living on Blackhawk Island was not easy. The unpredictable river sometimes rose and flooded houses along the riverbank, causing much damage and requiring tedious, messy salvaging and housecleaning when the water receded. During the spring each house had a boat tied near the front door for emergency transportation. Traveling there from town visitors notice that the houses grow smaller and smaller, then truly tiny. There is the poverty of oil barrels in front yards and junked cars, wheeless on jacks. When people first come upon the humble little cabin in which Lorine composed most of her early poems, they're struck by the simplicity of her home, yet she spoke with relish of the fullness of this environment —the "redwing blackbirds, willows, maples, boats, fishing (the smell of tarred nets) and the twittering and squawking noises from the marsh." As a poet, Niedecker never let her readers romanticize nature. A person standing on this dark and somewhat ominous spot knows why.

The property (now privately owned) is marked with a modest Wisconsin State Historical Marker, but even more poignant to the knowledgeable visitor is the small white hand pump outside her cabin. Lorine herself is buried at Union Cemetery, two and one-half miles away on Highway J, in the family plot next to her father and mother. Beside it is the much smaller headstone of Al Millen.

There's a special room in the Hoard's Museum down the block from the Dwight Foster Memorial Library on Merchant Avenue in downtown Fort Atkinson, which is now dedicated to Lorine Niedecker. The library maintains a collection that includes Lorine's personal books along with copies of her own published works, original manuscripts, interviews, pertinent periodicals, photographs, tapes and videos. Visitors are very welcome at both the library and the museum.

My life is hung up
in the flood
   a wave-blurred
      portrait

Don't fall in love
with this face —
   it no longer exists
      in water
         we cannot fish

To Make A Poem Your Own

An Appreciation of the Poetry of Lornie Niedecker

She was the daughter of a carp fisherman, who spent most of her life in obscurity writing on Fort Atkinson's Blackhawk Island. This year, 2003, marks the 100th anniversary of Lorine Niedecker's birth. Her reputation as a poet has been steadily increasing over the years, both in America and throughout the world, and with a new edition of her collected works from the University of California her standing is assured. Robert Creeley has said, "Lorine Niedecker proves a major poet of the twentieth century, just as Emily Dickinson was for the nineteenth. Bleak indeed that both should have been so curiously overwritten and ignored, when their work defined the time in which they lived with such genius."

NOVELS AND SHORT STORIES LOVE THE PAST. Maybe it's because they're longer, but each work seems to draw on a wider scope of experiences than an individual poem does. And that means the writer has to reach into experiences and observations that have happened over a longer period of time. It's why prose writers use the past tense. Poetry is more comfortable with the present. It is immediate, brief, intense. It may take advantage of poets' and readers' wide experiences, but it lives in the here and now. And no work exemplifies this better than the poetry of Lorine Niedecker.

Before taking a look at some of Lorine Niedecker's poems you might ask yourself three questions: "What do you bring to the reading of a poem (what are your expectations)?" "What is the experience of reading a poem as you do it, either aloud or to yourself?" And finally, "What do you take away from the poem — what stays with you after the experience has passed?"

There are all kinds of languages. That of science, for example, attempts to codify exactly as possible what we can know through our senses, or that of philosophy utilizes logic and abstractions of truth. We turn to fiction most often for the stories it offers of others and, by extension, how these stories apply to us. But what about the language of poetry? Most notably, we look to it for inspiration and consolation and expression of our feelings. Poems do this through extensive use of metaphor. The language of poetry lets us understand one entity (usually beyond our normal intellectual grasp, like *death* or *love*) in terms of another (usually a physical thing) that appeals more to our senses. All language is metaphoric — words stand for what they signify — but poetry not only uses this, it does it in a way that makes us appreciate the metaphoric process. The wonder of Lorine Niedecker's work is that since it is so "stripped down" it allows us to look at that process in a very pure form. For example, with *Something in the water* the words, as well as the water and the flower, are being swirled down, as though into a sink's drain, while we observe them.

> Something in the water
> like a flower
> will devour
>
> water
>
> flower

In a 1962 letter she wrote to Cid Corman, Lorine Niedecker said, "For me the sentence lies in wait — all those prepositions and connectives — like an early spring flood. A good thing my follow-up feeling has always been condense, condense." But the stripped-down form offers both advantages and disadvantages. When I look at today's contemporary poetry I see it appealing to people in two ways. First, there is a strong narrative quality to it. It is as if we are entering a miniature movie theater and the poet will tell us a story in a very prose-like way, though shorter and using some musical devices that make it stick in our memory (like a catchy theme song). I'm not criticizing this. In fact that's the way I write. I'm saying that people today enjoy being entertained and have re-discovered that poetry can do this. A second appeal is that it either plugs into our emotions easily or we can easily plug into the poet's. We like poems we can quote at a graduation, wedding or a funeral, poems that offer solace when we feel lonely or courage when we need to strengthen ourselves. Unfortunately, Lorine Niedecker's work is less entertaining for the passive reader and not as easily accessible for someone wanting to make a quick connection. Despite its simple appearance, it isn't easy.

So what advantages does her work offer instead? It forces us to slow down. To understand, rather than be understood. It reduces life to essentials in a way few things in our overwrought world do. It is demanding of us, but the result is we leave the experience with a sharpness and intensity that make our own existence more precise.

What that means in terms of approaching her poetry is that we need to set a different kind of expectation. For example, reading a page of prose might take two minutes, therefore reading a half a page would take one minute. But if that half page were one of Robert Frost's narrative poems laid out on a full piece of paper we would probably devote two or more minutes to it, even though it is half the number of words of a page of prose. That's because we give each line of poetry more "weight" and each word of its line more significance than we do to words of a line of prose. Niedecker gives us poems that use twenty percent of the words of the average Frost poem. Rather than zip by them, because they're short, we need to allow them as much time as we would a page of prose or a narrative poem. And attention shouldn't be just to the words. It needs to be to what they represent. More than any other poet, Lorine Niedecker stops us in our tracks. She forces us to block out all the distraction of our frantic, noisy world and experience life. If we are to get anything at all from her poems, it is first and foremost the gift of being *deliberately* in the moment. It's what Thoreau talked about in *Walden* and what the great teachers of the East have always reminded us of. Notice how small and elemental and real the world of *Popcorn-can cover* and *July, waxwings* are.

> Popcorn-can cover
> screwed to the wall
> over a hole
>   so the cold
> can't mouse in
>
>   •
>
> July, waxwings
> on the berries
> have dyed red
>   the dead
> branch

But for those of us not accustomed to reading poetry, how do we begin addressing a particular poem? Start by reading it aloud. Don't worry about meaning, or about vocally interpreting the words. Just read. Read it three or four times. This is a physical thing, letting our mouths shape the vowels and consonants, our breath breathing life into the words. It's like relishing the taste of food without verbalizing it, or gazing into the face of someone we love for the pure enjoyment that provides. As with a song, we first enter it through its melody, and once that is internalized, we become conscious of the meaning of its lyrics. Edward Hirsch claims, "Poems communicate before they are understood… Let the poem work in you as a human experience. Listen to the words and pay attention to the feelings (as opposed to meanings) they evoke." Reading a poem out loud is delighting in language; it's seeing how words taste.

Don't get bogged down in the rhythm or rhyme of a specific line in any poem. We want to simply be conscious of the patterns of sound behind the particular form the poem takes. This is like the enjoyment of jazz or classical music despite not being able to explain it in terms of musical notation (how restrictive that would be). But there are some things to be conscious of, such as the pause at the end of the line. Line breaks are like rests in music, and stanza breaks like rests that are twice as long. These are silences that are as important to the music as the words. You'll also be aware that you naturally stress some syllables of words more than others (this becomes the basis of meter in certain poetry). How does that pattern of inflection make you feel? Is there a rapid pace that makes you feel tense or a relaxed one that releases tension? Are these the rhythms of joy, love, despair or expectation? Generally, the words at the beginning and end of a line stand out a bit more than the others when you read them. The poet works with that, saving those positions for words whose meaning he or she wants emphasized. Also, the shorter the line and the shorter the poem, the tighter the language has to be. And rhyme? It goes back to the elemental pleasure we had reciting nursery rhymes as children. Better when subtle, rhyme is like hearing again a note that has already been struck. A poem doesn't include as exacting direction for the human voice as the notation of music, but its patterns and breaks do provide us with some direction. Best of all, a poem gives us the freedom to vocally make it uniquely our own.

When reading poetry aloud to ourselves, we all dream of sounding like James Earl Jones or like Gwyneth Paltrow in *Shakespeare in Love*. Here are a few hints: Slow down, breathe regularly. A person has more emotional range if he or she is not straining for volume or running out of breath. Recite the alphabet with exaggerated lip movement before you begin in order to limber up those muscles, and stand or sit straight so that your breathing is deep from your chest. Emphasize nouns and interpret verbs with more exaggeration than you would in regular speech (as Carl Sandburg said, make nouns echo and verbs quiver). Improve your delivery by recording it on a small cassette recorder, and listen to it carefully, just like you do when making a message for your telephone answering machine. Over time, your diction will magically improve. Try your hand reading *Hear* with interpretation.

> Hear
> where her snow-grave is
> the *You*
>   *ah you*
> of mourning doves

Poetry is also pictures. Before worrying about "what it means," identify the images of the poem. Most of these are visual, but notice how some appeal to our senses of touch, smell and even sometimes taste. They are moving pictures. Not only do we "move" through the poem as we read it, we move through physical images which themselves are in motion. These images are not exhaustive in description, but more often are suggested by one or two significant details. Images are what make poetry an experience rather than a description of an experience. And, readers are partners in creating completed images through the use of their own rich imaginations. Much as a painter creates the illusion of depth and perspective, the poet (with our help) creates a three-dimensional world from words on a two-dimensional page. And sometimes he or she does something even more amazing.

Some of the images are more than constructs of physical things. They also have a figurative meaning. We enter a world of correspondences with ties between our physical, emotional and spiritual levels of experience. And here "meaning" comes to signify making connections (real connections more powerful than fanciful thinking). Niedecker, Emily Dickinson and Frost, to mention a few poets whose work uses images as springboards, do this in two ways. First, by what they give us. For example, they choose one image over another, because it offers multiple levels of significance. Secondly, they do this by what they hold back—often the images when examined closely receive too much emphasis for their strictly literal value. They send us searching for meaning beyond the obvious.

> Fog-thick morning—
> I see only
> where I now walk. I carry
>   my clarity
> with me.

Paring back the number of words is not enough. It is the particular choices of what is presented that also makes Niedecker worth studying. Think about what you would or would not write about if you were a poet. On your deathbed what would you choose as the most poignant events of your life? We can compare Niedecker in her letters and in the eyes of those who knew her with the content of some of the most memorable work she wrote. Yet these are not often uplifting in the same way that a song or painting might be. That's because the troublesome things are most deeply ingrained. But even here she's selective. She writes about her working-class husband, but very little about her philandering father who "kept" another family. She writes about her deaf long-suffering mother, but not about Louis Zukofsky and Cid Corman whose friendships she courted over her lifetime. She writes about the child, Paul — Zukofsky's son—but (with one exception) not about the twins she would have had by him. Or is this true?

It seems to me that someone who lives a life of metaphors can also easily substitute one person for another. Her father and husband meld together, as do Lorine and her mother and the live child and dead children. Of course it's more complicated than that. But part of the fun of literature (despite disdain for it from the academic community) is this gossipy, quasi-psychoanalytic speculation. Niedecker's cryptic poetry is full of tantalizing clues and references that encourage this.

Wilderness

You are the man
You are my other country
and I find it hard going

You are the prickly pear
You are the sudden violent storm

the torrent to raise the river
to float the wounded doe

What is clear, however, is that she not only chose subjects that were difficult, but ones that have multiple layers of meaning and in which there is some kind of resolution (if from nothing else, from the beauty of that perfect match of content and form).

One suggestion many believe is a first step in grasping the full power of a poem is to paraphrase its meaning. In Niedecker's work there are at least three levels of meaning: 1) What literally is the physical subject of the poem and what is she focusing on with regard to it? 2) What is the meaning in terms of Niedecker's own life? There are enough biographical materials in this book to make a loose correlation between her life and her poems fairly simple. But a good poem is more than self-expression. It may begin as that, but it becomes art when a reader can enter it and make its experiences part of his or her own, and therefore... 3) Paraphrase what the poem says in terms of its meaning to you and your life. This last may not be as easy. But we are searching our own experiences and trying to find some patterns we share as human beings. Ultimately poetry makes us work harder, but we will find the results all the more satisfying.

Some of these last two levels of meaning involve subjects that we cannot deal with easily using regular prose. We turn to metaphor. It describes one thing in terms of another, but these are very seldom of equal importance. One side of the comparison is physical, specific ... can be grasped through the senses (and poetry uses more than our intellect). We hear its sounds and see its images. We even smell and taste it through our imaginations in a way that is often star- tlingly vivid. It's true that other forms of writing use these same devices, but never with the intensity of poetry. In fact, they seem to define a piece of writing as poetry, even more than its form on the page. But the other side of the metaphoric comparison, though no less real, is less substantial to our senses, but more profound. And this is where poetry's real strength lies. As Marianne Moore once said, "The power of the visible is in the invisible." With poetry, through the visible, we are emotionally, intellectually, even physically, grappling with *love, death, success, defeat, the future, our past*—the forces of life.

One reason poets select some subjects and not others is that they feel they can wrestle with them using the tools of poetry. When the poem is successful, the transformation process leads to some sort of an understanding at the intellectual, sensual and musical levels that proves satisfying. Lesser poetry tacks on a moral. Greater poetry, like that of Niedecker, preserves the complexity of the subject. It doesn't simplify the subject, but with ordinary words celebrates its density. Though her poems may appear simple, they aren't. But that doesn't mean they don't lead to some sort of resolution. When people refer to the redemptive quality of art, they mean that even though the subject may be depressing, there is a hopefulness about being able to express it that gives us power and allows us to move beyond that depression. It may not be the same as a solution to a problem, but even an expression of something unpleasant, if done with grace and efficiency, can take our breath away. Sometimes this is done by as little as a single word or phrase at the end of a Niedecker poem that surprises us, confronts our expectations and makes us re-examine the poem's theme all over again.

> I walked
> on New Year's Day
>
> beside the trees
> my father now gone planted
>
> evenly following
> the road
>
> Each
>   spoke

Niedecker's poetry is not a journey to another place. It takes us neither forward nor backward in time. Rather, it's a journey into nearness and immediacy. If we take the time and the effort to make some of these poems our own, they can awaken us and make us more fully aware of our own lives. Thoreau wrote, "Men esteem truth remote, in the outskirts of the system, behind the farthest star, before Adam and after the last man. In eternity there is indeed something true and sublime. But all these times and places and occasions are now and here. God himself culminates in the present moment, and will never be more divine in the laps of all the ages. And we are enabled to apprehend at all what is sublime and noble only by the perpetual instilling and drenching of the reality that surrounds us." We understand what Thoreau means through his writing. We experience it for ourselves in the poetry of Lorine Niedecker.

— John Lehman, January 3, 2003

Ten Practical Suggestions on
How to Make a Poem Your Own

1. Can you recall a moment in your own life that seemed unusually intense, where you were more aware than usual of being entirely in the here and now?

2. Read through a selection of poems and pick one that you especially relate to. In your own words tell how it expresses the essence of its subject.

3. Other poets and writers take the opposite approach to that of Lorine Niedecker. They write long work overflowing with detail. What advantages does that offer you as a reader?

4. Take a particular poem that attracts you for some initial reason and read it out loud three times without thinking about any deeper meaning. Try to imagine you were the poet and the experience of the poem is coming to you as you read; and try to communicate that to someone hearing it (even if there isn't anyone besides yourself).

5. Make it easy on yourself and pick a short poem that resonates with how you often feel. Now memorize it. When you do this, you're using the same lip movements and breath the poet did when he or she first said the poem while writing it. If you feel up to it, try memorizing another.

6. Take the rhythms of a particular poem and try to substitute word for word your own subject on your own theme. If there's an adjective, noun, verb, conjunction, verb, noun, do the same in the same order for your own piece. This is the equivalent of art students' copying the work of a master in order to understand the choices and challenges the original painter made.

7. Find a poem that particularly captures your interest and give its literal meaning, the meaning you think it has in terms of the poet's life and how it's meaningful to you. Now take a poem by Niedecker that initially you don't find appealing and try to do the same thing.

8. Of course a poem is more than levels of meaning. Think of it as a story, a painting and a piece of music. Choose a poem and tell it as if it were a story. Then describe its images as if they were a picture or series of pictures in a gallery. Finally, what are the musical devices the poem uses — certain sounds and rhythms — and what popular, classical or jazz pieces does it bring to mind?

9. Another way of penetrating poetry is to take two poems that seem to be on similar themes and compare and contrast them both in terms of form and content. Try to decide what affects you and how, and don't be afraid to have strong preferences.

10. The ultimate way to appreciate and show appreciation for a writer is to do an informal presentation about him or her to others not familiar with the writer's work. Why not ask for fifteen minutes of your next book or writer discussion group's meeting to do this for Lorine Niedecker's or some other poet's work? Present a few of the poems as you've come to value them, and don't hesitate to give your personal reactions. Who knows, this might encourage others to follow your lead.

Consider at the outset:
to be thin for thought
or thick cream blossomy

Many things are better
flavored with bacon

Sweet Life, My Love:
didn't you ever try
this delicacy — the marrow
in the bone?

And don't be afraid
to pour wine over cabbage

John Lehman

John Lehman is the founder and original publisher of *Rosebud*. He is the poetry editor of the *Wisconsin Academy Review*, the managing partner of Zelda Wilde Publishing, editor/publisher of the free Madison street-quarterly, *Cup of Poems with a Side of Prose*, and founding member of the Prairie Fire Poetry Quartet. His collections of poetry include *Shrine of the Tooth Fairy*, *Dogs Dream of Running* and *Shorts: Brief Wisconsin Poems*. John grew up in Chicago but for the past fifteen years has lived with his wife, Talia Schorr, and their four dogs in Rockdale, Wisconsin, fifteen minutes from Blackhawk Island, where Lorine Niedecker was born 100 years ago. They have four grown children: Karl, Pam, Renee and Rachel.

———

Poet's Work

Grandfather
　advised me:
　　Learn a trade

I learned
　to sit at desk
　　and condense

No layoff
　from this
　　condensery

———

Lorine Niedecker, 1903 - 1970